The Sons of Darkness
and the Sons of Light

Ian Parks

Crooked Spire Press

First published in 2025
by Crooked Spire Press
Barlborough
Chesterfield
Derbyshire

www.crookedspirepress.com

email: crookedspirepress@mail.com

Edited and typeset by Tim Fellows
Proofreading by Fiona Fellows

Printed by John Brailsford Printers,
30 Rawmarsh Hill, Rotherham, S62 6EU.
www.brailsfordprinters.com

ISBN 978-1-0684229-3-5

Contents

For my friend Bob Horne

Jesus of Mexborough

He came out of the wilderness
with nothing on his feet;
he came out of the wilderness
to walk the shuttered street.
After forty days of fasting
he ate till he was full
then slaked his thirst by downing
a few pints in the Bull.

He pushed against the pit wheel
and tried to make it turn;
he said to the schoolchildren
There's much you must unlearn.
He went into the car park
and tore the pay-point down;
he said *All parking should be free*
here in your own hometown.

He went into the parish church
and threw the hymn books out.
I'll come back in judgement
is what they heard him shout.
Get up from your knees he said
You mustn't call me Lord.
Don't think I came to bring you peace –
I came to bring a sword.

He kicked the crutches from the lame
and told them they could walk;
he went into the bingo hall
and joined them in their talk.
He cleared the shelves in Poundland
and gave Greggs' food away.
He told the jobless and the poor
You shouldn't have to pay.

He went into the marketplace,
his eyes they brightly burned;
left takings scattered on the floor
and tables overturned.
They chased him through the local pub,
they said he was deranged.
They chased him till they had no breath
but something in them changed.

Someone sent for the police,
their sirens cut the air
and though they searched the town for him
they found he wasn't there.
When the crowds caught up with him
he told them *It's your loss.*
You'll find me on the underpass
still carrying my cross.

Winter Hill

I met her at the top of Winter Hill,
a rucksack slung over one arm.
I noticed her, she didn't notice me.
The path was steep and rutted, filled with rain
and when she asked me if I had a wish
I wished I might be young again;

to lean on the unmended fence,
to look down in the valley and to see
each footstep of the way I came
past slanting cottages and sinking farm,
the tall graves of the hidden dead
keeping their secret safe from harm

and feel the climb required no recompense.
I made a promise I couldn't fulfil
there on the hillside with its frozen name.
These are the only words we said.
Before the coming of the storm
the trees are restless and the roots are still.

Miners Cutting Trees Down in the Middle of the Strike

A misty morning and you wake
to hear the bite of axes in the dawn.
The miners turn up at first light
to chop down branches from the winter trees

and take them home because they have no coal,
their wives and children shivering.
It is as if the sun's been taken down,
bled out and not returned.

The trees are on the edge of an Estate –
a family who owned the mines
before the pits were nationalised.
The shrunk horizon pulls them in.

The air is filled with sawdust
and will soon be filled with blood
because the raw policemen come
with batons and in armoured cars.

And later they will warm scuffed hands
and laugh as the world begins to freeze
in a corner of the schoolyard
where the logs are stacked and burned.

The Dogs of Whitby

The dogs of Whitby have a hungry look.
They linger in the alleys after dark.

One midnight when the fishing boats were out
I took a short-cut through the empty town –

Cook's statue and the whale-rib monument,
the fisherwomen whispering *Come soon.*

Somewhere below the abbey steps
two dogs were worrying a bone.

It had the features of a dream, a non-event
which made me say *It isn't finished yet.*

We'll wake at the same instant and you'll hear
the dogs of Whitby howling at the moon.

Three

All three are wren-like, vigilant,
their heads turned slightly from the world
and far off as if listening to the sound

of wind bending the trees back on the moors
or the grey slabs of the gravestones
shifting, upended, tilting to the ground

but sharp, determined, self-contained,
all different, different, different but the same –
without the slightest fear and with no doubt.

Alert, inquisitive, their needle-point eyes.
Their restless hands are folded, white.
The canvas is too small. It struggles to contain

three spirits straining to be free:
the sisters with their bright intensity
on a Sabbath Day of tireless wind and rain,

a meagre fire struggling in the grate.
The absinthe stain dividing them
is their brother who tried to paint himself out.

The Snow Plough

The snow plough laboured up the hill
    of our abandoned town,
        tossing the freshly-fallen drifts

onto the far side of the road
    where soon our boots would sully them.
        The newspapers were right:

the last of the day made a narrow slit
    between the rooftops and the loaded sky
        where everything came down.

The amber lights were flashing
    as it took the final bend
        and you, my son, were singing

as the snow plough came abreast –
    quite loudly, unexpectedly
        in the way that children sing

not to be heard or understood
    but to raise a voice up from the falling snow
        for nothing but the sake of it.

Death Goes Riding with Hank Williams in the Back Seat of a Car

A 1952 Olympic Blue
Cadillac Convertible to be precise.
The driver didn't see her getting in
and never saw her getting out again
but on the way to Oak Hill

where the road was made of ice
and a blizzard threw
a white sheet on the screen,
the New Year cold and shivering
on the way to one more show

he caught the tang of cheap perfume
and cheaper bootleg gin.
He stopped his car for gasoline
and found she wouldn't start.
In the back seat he'd been listening

to the local radio: his own songs
thin and tinny as she gave a final kiss
somewhere in West Virginia
and somewhere in between
Lost Highway and *Your Cheating Heart*.

The Splinter

The shell exploded
high above his head
among the branches
of the summer trees,
his tank disabled and askew
there in the sunken lane –
his poems unwritten and unsaid
as he ducked for shelter in the shade.
I went there once to see the view
of open farmland and, far off,
the red-tiled villages and spires
which were the last thing that he knew.
He froze there for an instant
but an instant was enough.
The demon at his shoulder
shouted *now*, he dropped down
on his knees without a word,
his body white, immaculate
except for the splinter
that came slicing in
from out of nowhere, quivering
and cut the spinal cord.

Sunk Island

If you take me to Sunk Island
as you often said you would
you needn't bring me back.
What was once a promise

has now become a threat.
The man who casts his line
into the slow, grey tidal river
is a friend of mine;

the girl who hangs her wedding dress
between two posts to the sky,
the boy who wheels his bicycle
among the dunes but never rides,

and the sullen-eyed birdwatchers
who nod but fail to speak
are also of my kind.
They've turned their backs on England

and left it far behind –
its pebble-blasted cottages
and fields of oil-seed rape.
If you take me to Sunk Island

you needn't bring me back.
You can leave me high and dry
on the road to nowhere except Paull
where the Meridian passes through

to watch the sun sink low and set
in a place uncertain,
caught between two tides
among the mud-flats, changing shape.

The Paper Crown

Richard of York Gave Battle in Vain

Shakespeare made him eloquent in death;
the sure iambics rolling in like waves
to break on the shore of his grief.
I don't think they gave him chance to speak,
the northern lords who cut him down
between the high ground and the river trees;
the Flower of Craven and his kind.
If time permits I'll take you to the spot –
a rusted railing and a stone-cold plinth
where they hacked off his noble head
and crowned him with a paper crown
high on the walls of Micklegate Bar
so York could overlook the town of York.
History forgets the ones who tried and failed.
Remember him – if you remember him at all –
for being the king he never was
and the colours of the rainbow in his fall.

The Golden Mile

That's where you got started my father said,
pointing across the sand-blown track
to a first-floor room in a Blackpool hotel.
My mother pulled her collar up
to hide the blush that spread into her cheeks.

It must have been their honeymoon –
the biting spring of 1958,
the Tower Ballroom where they danced,
the chiffon dress that she would keep
until the day she died; my father in his shirtsleeves

at the window, looking out,
smoking a Woodbine as the trams
completed their circuit of the Golden Mile
and me nothing more than a twinkle
in his dark, proverbial eye.

Peace Conference

It is beneath my dignity
to wait for hours like this.
I huddle closer to the stove
and hear the snip, snip, snip.
My overcoat is heavy with the rain.

Go to Sheffield Pablo.
It will do your image good.
And get a haircut while you're there.
The delegates are waiting for my speech
but while I'm sitting in the queue

I come up with the image of a dove –
a few bold curves, my signature,
the suggestion of spread wings.
Once I'm sure it needs nothing more
I set it free in flight.

Get them to do something
with your fringe they said.
It makes you look like Hitler.
I stare at the mirror opposite
and think they might be right.

The Final Firing of the Year

Not because she doesn't care
about the outcome of the current war
and not because distraction can be found
in the thud of clay and the shine of glaze

there in her brick studio, its corrugated roof –
but because the more she concentrates
the more she understands
the dead lost in the rubble have no voice.

She heats the kiln until it glows pure white,
until the hidden meaning comes more clear.
Her eye is sharp, her mind is sharper still.
The radio refuses, the signal comes and goes

as she begins to number all her days.
She rinses the red slip from her bare hands.
A light is shining through the belt of trees.
This is the final firing of the year.

Milner Place in Heaven

By now I know you will have found
your own seat at the far end of the bar
where you will roll an endless cigarette,

adjust your glasses and begin to read.
A crowd will gather round to hear
the tall tales that you used to tell

about the sea so still you couldn't breathe
or winds so high they shook you when they roared.
But most of all it was the ones you lost –

the ones you knew you couldn't save
and ploughed on resolutely through the spray.
Captain, you're now exactly as you were

before you ended landlocked on the shore,
before the huge wave crashed on deck
and washed you overboard.

Trespass

It takes just one gamekeeper and his gun
to scare a pair of walkers from the land.
It takes a pack of growling dogs
to stop them in their tracks, to see them off

and send them back the way they came.
It only takes a crude, hand-painted sign
to keep the Sunday ramblers at bay.
But when they met in thousands as they did

in that forgotten lull between the wars –
the shop girls and the mill hands
and the pit lads from the mines –
the unexpected morning when they came

to swarm up Jacob's Ladder and its steep stone stairs
there was nothing they could do but give them back
that place of light and air and rapid cloud:
the open ground that was already theirs.

The Snow Storm

The movement of the carriage woke me up.
It seemed we were between two old regimes –
the way that Europe used to be
before the wars tore it apart.

I took your hand and lifted up the blind.
The train was crawling through the storm
and all the little villages we passed
were huddled in the silence, dimly lit.

Your hair cascaded through my dreams
and then, as if you'd read my mind
you said *Is there another love poem in your heart?*
I smiled and answered *This is it.*

Shooting Stars

Here we have no shooting stars
to leave a trail across the northern skies.
Three hundred years of smoke and grime
obscured them from our sight.
It doesn't stop us looking though:

the streets are filled with hopeful souls
who gather there to see
the stricken angels fall.
Your cities have polluted
our dark regions with their light.

Likewise, you will not listen when we say
remove your high-speed railway from our door
and stop the choking fume of cars;
give back to us our clear cold winter night
and let our children see the shooting stars.

The Rescue

Thirty miles west of the Golden Gate
they chanced upon her – bigger than their boat –
drifting aimless on the sea, her jaws
clamped tight together with a nylon thread.

They took their curved knives from their belts
and slipped over the side
despite the white sharks circling for the kill.
From dawn to dusk they disentangled her –

rolling her body over on the swell,
treading water for an hour or so
then clambering back on deck.
And in the end the sea grew still.

What he remembers is her patient eye
that watched him as he worked:
unpicked the frayed end of the stubborn knot,
cut through the final cord and set her free.

Moon Landing

The night they landed on the moon
my father woke me up and took me down
to watch the grainy figures on the screen
as they kicked up the moon dust with their boots.

The flag they planted didn't cast
a shadow as they came and went
to take possession of a thing you can't possess.
The artists and the poets always knew

it lay beyond the limit of our reach,
secure in its own otherness.
My father was no poet but he felt it was a crime
to trespass where no human foot should tread.

And so it was he threw the curtains wide
to show its pure and naked loveliness
which made us pause, switch off the rented set
and gaze up at the real thing instead.

The Tower

We slogged up from the valley floor.
Each time we looked up from the path
the hill fort occupied a different space

as if four thousand years of being there
had given it the power to evade
a fixed approach, a single view.

Only when the tower reared above
did it become a thing of solid stone –
a place that you could reach and touch

where image and perception were the same.
You went inside and climbed up to the top.
I thought of every step you took –

the stone stairs slanting and the light
as it came in to open up the rooms.
Then you were leaning on the rail

above the undulating moors,
a figure I could hardly recognise
waving down and calling out my name.

Mermaid's Hair

In the lull before the storm
I took my lover by the arm
to see the mermaid's hair
that floated smooth and aqueous
over the pebbles of the weir.
We were no more than seventeen

and soon, I knew, she'd have to go –
but I was glad to have her there,
slipping hot feet from her shoes
to let the long strands swirl and stream
her ankles green on white.
There were dragonflies that summer

and they darted all about us
as she untangled her numbed feet
and rested them on the scorched stones to dry.
There was the future in the moment
and in those wet prints as they disappeared
the first poems of my life.

The Decembrists

After the revolution failed
they shrank back to the attic rooms
where it had all begun —
the flaking plaster and an uncontested view
across a city grown indifferent under snow,

the high white ceilings and the chandeliers;
the bridge across the Neva occupied.
History would happen somewhere else.
The lovers spoke in whispers
on the stunned street corners now

and in the square where many of them died
the troops who came to wash the blood away
were underfed, unpaid, and bored.
Civilians in long-tail coats and furs
edged out into the daylight cautiously

from hiding places, haunted afternoons
where lamps were lit in the frozen air
and all the instruments of state restored.
She would go with him into exile
on the next slow carriage out.

He faltered on the final step
and turned his collar up against the cold.
The New Year bells were ringing
as he watched the sun ascend
and placed a frostbit hand in hers.

Moonlight on an Unadopted Road

I'd like to live my life out
on an unadopted road,
watching the rain fill in
the unadopted cracks

and all the small eruptions of neglect
that scar the tarmac
just outside the door
and smile and not to care.

I would want you with me
when the moonlight visited
to place a candle on the windowsill
and throw another fleece

over the bed. The road itself
would have no name:
a blank sign on the corner
to confuse the passerby.

I would not be yours
and you would not be mine,
taking another book down
from the creaking shelf.

The moon would disentangle
all its fading light
where nettles huddle at the fence
and names don't matter anymore

and there, together, love might grow
in the silences between
the distant hum of traffic
and the kettle's plaintive whine.

Marston Moor

I've come to the edge of the arable land
where the straight swords are crossing on the map
in a time of indecision and a time of change.
There, on the far side of the swale,

a wall of pikes held back the royalist horse
and where the thin hedge peters out
men from the same country shot them down.
Some say it's for the best the houses come

to sink their deep foundations in the soil.
For now they're out of sight and out of range.
So let the dead lie undisturbed
where every rise and dip in that bare ground

marks out the places where they fell
and come here when the sun is sinking low
over the scrub, the footpaths and the open plain
in a time of indecision and a time of change.

The Wiper

I have the backseat to myself
although the tartan rug scratches my knees.
The rapid wiper sweeps across the screen,
obliterates a sudden wash of rain
that fills again with each successive wave.
The fine white line recedes

on what I now know is a motorway.
My mother pours hot oxtail from a flask;
my father hums the rhythm of the night.
It is The Bachelors I think, their song
about the long road leading home
and the smile of the girl like a guiding light –

but the radio's a whisper, far away.
This is the final stretch of amber glow
before we reach our door
and soon the decade will remove its mask.
I'm at the very edge of sleep.
There won't be many times like these.

Thatcher

The day they buried Thatcher
I was standing in the rain
in Goldthorpe where the closures hit them hard.
Someone had made an effigy

and dragged it from the yard –
her handbag trailing and the wig askew.
They pushed her in a rusting pram
past empty pubs and crumbling schools

to where a bonfire waited
on the recreation ground.
And when they lit the newspapers
a groan erupted from the crowd:

men wept with joy, the children danced
and all the women cheered.
The mask slipped first then melted.
The smoke was black and stung my eyes.

Jarrow March

Instead of revolution we have rain:
it seeps into the English soil
and permeates our lives.

Some stayed at home and made the pit wheel turn,
some manned the barricades in Spain
and came back changed by what they saw –

the bombed-out cities and the ruined squares,
or they put on their overcoats and caps
and took the long road south to Parliament.

The newsreel shows them smiling,
singing songs they'd learned by heart
from marching in a different kind of war,

despite the downpour and the roughness of the road.
Each had a Woodbine dangling from his mouth.
They came back empty-handed and unheard.

And now the last of them is dead
I look out on the dripping rain
and wonder what it meant

or what it means to live without a voice
in this bland, slipshod democracy
we need to reinvent.

The Well

They sank the well
before they built the house.
They built the house
before they made the lane.

She cursed the well
and set fire to the house
before she went insane.
Now well and house

and wood and lane
exist in close proximity
as if in waiting there for me
to turn up in the rain.

Two rotting shutters
keep the well secure,
held by a padlock
and a rusting chain.

Jack Kerouac at Desolation Peak

Sixty days of solitude
above the North Cascades.
His lookout is a shack on stilts
and when the mist comes rolling in
the peaks are islands in a milky sea.
At nine the radio crackles into life:
it is the only voice he hears
except his own reminding him

of city sidewalks, driving rain,
the pulse of neon and a purple sign
where jazz invents
its language in the dark
before the signal falters first then fades.
From time to time a wisp of smoke
distracts him from his lines.
He picks up his binoculars and stares –

but one quick blink convinces him
that too much looking can deceive
and make a thing occur.
The view from here is sacred,
weighted and unchanged. He rolls
a cigarette and strikes a match.
The pines release their scent.
There won't be any fires on his watch.

The Seam

When I was ten my father took me down
so I could see the coal face where he'd spent
the best part of his life, plying his pick

and shovel in the three-foot seam.
The thing I feared most was the heat –
the stripped men sweating in the dark

and the splintered props when they gave way and creaked.
Nothing I'd known could be worse than this.
On his first day, just seventeen

they took a penknife to his arm
and scratched the letters of his name,
rubbed coal dust in to make a crude tattoo

that quivered on the bedsheets
decades later when he died.
I knew I'd never go back to that place.

On his last day he poured the water out
forever from his tin canteen
and said goodbye to everything:

his work mates, the blind pit ponies
and the gleaming wall of sheer black rock
which he bent close to kiss.

I Meet You at the Horses

I meet you at the horses where they graze,
picking the burs out from a matted mane.
Two grey foals and a piebald mare
nod gently at the fence, their hot breath

rising in the air and mingling with yours:
four spirits shimmering in the autumn haze
that rises from the river where it flows.
I know you'd love to ride her, set her free

over the far horizon with its belt of trees.
Instead you press her huge head to your breast
and stroke her forelock, watch her eyes
as she succumbs to darkness and they close.

There is nothing but this patch of open ground,
the bridge I cross to find you here –
your spirit shining through you as you turn;
your dreams through which the horses pound.

Alfred Jewel

When they came to drain the marsh
a clod of muddy earth broke free.
They rinsed it under the cold pump
and held it to the light.

One rubbed the surface with his thumb
and called the others over to make out
a figure underneath the clouded glass
embedded like a kingfisher in ice –

the orb and sceptre in his hands,
an opening where the pointer used to be
and round the rim in the Saxon tongue
King Alfred had me made.

Ferry Boat Halt

And then there was the time
my cousin rang me up
to tell me that Duane Eddy was in town.
I'd catch him jamming at the Ferry Boat
if I moved quick enough.
I pulled my jeans on, crossed the tracks,

turned the street corner when I heard
the deep, distinctive twang
that set ten-thousand guitars quivering.
Except this was South Yorkshire not LA
and he was older, bent to his guitar
between one booking and the next

as if it was the only thing to do.
No amplification, no support.
He'd called in on a quiet afternoon
and in the taproom with no fuss
ordered a whisky without ice
and never came again.

Wherever you are Eddy
I wish you an endless road
for the hour you spent in Mexborough
as the barmaid cleared away
and for the song you left for us
as you were passing through.

Samphire

Low tide is the time to gather it
when the waves are in abeyance
and the gulls are sweeping low.
Go out across the miles of hard-ribbed sand –

the brittle shingle cracking at your tread
and tug the shallow roots until they give.
Fill up your basket as the sun descends
over narrow-slitted pill-boxes,

the sand banks and the dunes.
Move quick before the tide returns
and pause before you go
to see the samphire spreading yellow-green

along the length of that abandoned shore.
Carry it back to this landlocked place,
blanch it with water, eat your fill
and tell me if you taste the sea.

Jerry

The road began for you when you were five
in Ferriday one Sunday after church.
Your father showed you middle C –
the only lesson you would ever need
when something deep inside you came alive.

In Hamburg, at the Star Club where you played
you slicked your hair back, flirted with the crowd
and hit the keys so hard
the owners thought they'd break.
We expected you to die before old age:

to exit on the beat and not to fade.
I saw you near the end with a white cane,
shambling from the wings onto the stage.
Waiting for your spirit to be freed
you soared above the chaos you had made.

Butterfly House

With wings the colour of your eyes
and your pale hands outspread
the huge exotic butterflies –

short-lived under the glass
will never flicker far
from the white chrysalis they've shed.

The sugar in the basin of your palm
has tempted them to come
through giant fronds and artificial air

to settle on your breast.
You should be wearing crinoline or lace
with damp collecting sweet and hot

there in the small of your back
but the world has turned
too many times since then.

The butterflies are poised and innocent.
Blink once and they're forever gone.
They leave no shadow on your face.

Grendel's Dam

Paul Goodman, I remember you –
we had a desk together in Year Three.
And more than you I still recall
the illustrated *Beowulf* we shared

and Grendel's Mother, Grendel's Dam
an inky sprawl across the open page,
plucking her victims from the mere
and plunging to her underwater lair.

Although I wasn't there to see you drown
swimming in the river, in the heat
I knew you were entangled in her hair.
It was her icy fingers dragged you down.

Bleaklow

We came across the rusted fuselage
and one wing lodged in the peaty earth
like a roof tile in the lawn after a storm.

But nothing should surprise you
on that burned out plateau
where a war plane lost control

and spiralled down,
the splintered wreckage spread over a mile.
No one saw the fire explode

when it hit the neutral ground
or heard the pilot in distress.
Seventy years of plunderers

in search of souvenirs
have failed to pick it clean:
I prised a piece of dashboard from the soil

and held it to the light.
If it was one of ours or one of theirs
is a question that is asked there less and less.

Effigy

I sat beside her for an hour or more
there in the recess of the empty church.
Outside it was almost winter
and the branches of a stricken tree
tapped and scraped against the coloured glass.
Six centuries she'd lain there, carved from stone,

her eyes fixed on the rafters and her coif
draped snugly round her chiselled head.
Six centuries of leaf-fall, sunlight, snow –
the incremental shadows every night
as they inched across the damp-flagged floor,
the sound of evensong and psalms.

Six centuries of peace and distant wars.
I brushed a cobweb from her face
and lit a candle at her pointed feet.
If I believed I would have knelt and prayed.
No one could tell me who she was or why
she held her own heart in her open palms.

Lesbos

There are life jackets on the beach.
They float in on the tide,
washed up by its endless push and pull.
Each one brought an immigrant
who came ashore or died,

rearing a wall across the bay
as Leonidas did to keep the Persians out.
Sometimes they make a pile of them
and put them to the torch
in a new ritual of ash and flame.

The black smoke rises in the air.
The gods must know about it
but the gods have gone elsewhere.
There are life jackets on the beach
because the sea is full.

War Effort

My grandfather came home on leave
to find his pots and pans were gone.
Outside the air-raid shelter
with its corrugated roof
he lit a Woodbine, stood alone.

Likewise, the railings and the gate –
all commandeered and carted off
to forge the bombs they said we'd need
to make the final push.
He tuned the wireless, waited for a sign

as the contents of his kitchen
screamed and hurtled down
on women, children, and old men:
the unsuspecting citizens
of Dresden and Cologne.

Heron

The day after my great-grandmother died
I saw a heron on the riverbank.
Towards the end she had the second sight.

I was no more than eight or nine.
Bolt upright in the brass and bolstered bed
she looked at me and called me to her side.

The heron was impassive
with its hinged and folded wings,
refused to scare until I came so near

I felt the air displaced by its brisk flight
as if it knew there was no need to fear
there in the shallows, in the mist-filled air.

And now, it seems, I never think of her
unless, alone, I chance upon her kind –
grey in the morning where the willows bend

intent on something I don't understand,
absorbed by how the silent river flows –
wrapped in her shroud of solitude.

The Pendant

I was sitting in the sacred grove
that fronts the entrance to the cave
in Delphi where Apollo spoke
before the Christians drove the god away.
A sharp glint in the corner of my eye

and there it was: a green moon,
tarnished glass, hanging by a single thread
from the bare branches of an olive tree.
I took it down and brought it back;
I held it to the sun and saw

the fallen stones awash with verdant light.
And now you press it to your breast.
It once was mine and now is yours to keep.
These are the inner workings of the world:
this is the way the gods behave.

The Cab

The cab was waiting on the kerb
outside the Albert and the night was black.
I can't remember now for sure
exactly what had brought me there
or where exactly I was bound
but the strange new music I'd just found
was playing in my head.

It was late in Huddersfield
and the rain was running down my face.
Geoff Hattersley and Milner Place
were laughing as they wound
the window down and said
There's room for one more poet in the back.

The Nephilim

They spent all weekend in the pub
before the pits were closed:
bruisers, fellers, crude intemperate men

who took exception if you caught their eye.
Beer by the gallon, Park Drives by the score,
discoursing loudly on the racing form

there in the tap room where the lights were low,
these were the mighty ones of old –
offspring of angels and working girls,

of random couplings in the fields –
who had no children of their own
and perished in the waters of the Flood,

their wad-filled wallets floating on the swell:
their scuffed, raw knuckles turning white,
their oaths unspoken and their teeth of gold.

The Snowing Globe

When we were young it wasn't hard
to stand inside the snowing globe

and let the shaken flakes swirl from the dome.
It wasn't hard to shift the paperweight

from palm to palm, and live inside the glass –
small figures in a less than perfect world.

The gods will not allow it:
soon the glass goes rolling on the floor,

the brittle moment passes
and we see things as they really are

from the cold outside looking in
where a blizzard is a blizzard

and the language that we use
is confounded, compromised,

not knowing the last word we'll whisper
as it slips out of our hand.

Horse Fair

Lost son, I met your double
in a distant market town.
I was there to watch the horses
racing through the narrow streets;
to see them gather on the shingle bank
and swim in the Eden River.
And there you were as if by chance
in among the milling press,
the smell of horses, their hot flanks.
The mares and foals and stallions
all blinking in a summer haze
and tethered there together.
He had you off by heart:
the freckle where your shoulder met your neck,
the calf-lick on your crown,
his hands, his eyes the same.
The child you were was looking up at me,
asking if it was all right to stroke
the soft pink muzzle nudging at the fence;
to reach across the space between and touch.
The bare-back riders plunged into the stream.
The sun stood still and blazing.
And *Yes* I nodded *yes it is*
while trying not to speak your name.

The Pilgrimage of Grace

They crouch low in the wetlands
inundated by the rain –
a rebel army of ten thousand souls,
each man an island in the washed-out plain.
The careful telling of the beads.

If you stand at Scawsby Leys you'll see
the landscape laid to rest
under a layer of tarmac and regret:
the car park, supermarket, and the school.
You could invoke five hundred years

of history to explain
why nothing happened
in that fallen world of stunted tree stumps
and indifferent spires,
the soldiers scarcely breathing

as they wait to go to war.
Not much has changed since then.
There will be no battle here today –
only the stillness and the distant hum
of traffic on the motorway;

the promises made by the king
which he would later break;
the men returning to their washed-out homes
dispersing, as the clouds disperse,
to gather once again.

Henry Moore Notebook

Coal Miner Carrying Lamp

I'll be telling this to someone else
years after the event –
how sheer the black that fell on us,

the black and then the heat
running between our shoulder blades
and streaming down our backs.

No falling roof, no accident,
no scrambling for the lamps
but something pressing heavy on our lids,

the props about to split
and heaving his own body from the face
a man of coal and candlewax.

Boys at the Pit Head

Four heads, four faces
and an inky watercolour wash
instead of winter sky:
four helmets from another war
and lamps that float on darkness
then go down, the cage
in the background plummeting.
One alert, inquisitive;
another his own skeleton.
They should be back in school.
They will raise hell up
from the hollow ground.
They will taste victory and defeat.
They will be boys
until the day they die.

Fats Waller Visits Sheffield on his Birthday

He doesn't have that long to live
so when the show is over
and the Empire is shut down

he goes back to his hotel and tries to sleep.
Incongruous in his huge fur coat
and jaunty bowler hat

he whistles as he walks the city streets,
three thousand miles from Harlem
where the jazz flows sweet and hot.

His spats splash in the puddles,
a roll-up hangs from his lower lip
and in his head the notes are echoing.

Out of the drizzle and the dawn
the pure song of a thrush.
But soon the bombs will start to fall

and the gardens where he sits will be
reduced to rubble and to mud.
There in his room he smiles and sips

straight whisky from a painted glass,
stares at the piano, rolls his eyes
and writes the first few bars of *Honey Hush*.

Griffin

I met you at the corner of the street
pulling your collar up against the wind
in Hull where all the promises were made.

We found a corner in the nearest pub
where couples leaned together in the gloom
and drank. The city kept its secret hid:

the jetty where the ferry plied its trade
before they spanned the river with a bridge.
I remember, Tony, how the hours fell

in the Minerva's ship-shape snug –
you flicking through the pages of your book
and reading your impassioned poems to me

as if there were no others in the room
as rain fell on the mud-banks at the door.
And sometimes when I glimpse your shade

I catch the tilt of light upon your skull,
the day's bitter intensity
and out there where we never turned to look

the Estuary becoming the North Sea.

The Sparrow

After the Anglo-Saxon

Or take, for example, the flight
    of a sparrow through the winter night
into the bright-lit chamber where we sit.
    It enters from the darkness,
exits where the torch-light ends

there in the rafters high above our heads.
    Outside is blizzard, chaos,
nothingness. We see it and forget –
    but it takes with it in its reckless flight
our first-born children, our true friends,

mother, sister, father, brother, wife.
    We look up from our feasting,
the mead flows free again,
    the bard picks up the lost thread of his song.
This is all we know of life.

At the Miners' Memorial

He said that when the sun goes down
at Caphouse on a winter afternoon
or when it rises with the mist
the discs are vibrant as stained glass:

amber, purple, lilac, green –
and on each disc the date and name
of someone loved and lost
lodged in a curving metal seam;

a way of living laid to rest
among the winding gear and rust.
And where the train line peters out
on the fringes of a thin, impoverished wood

the pin-point glow is an abandoned cigarette.
There at the top of the narrow lane
I'm waiting for my father's ghost
to meet me in the rain.

The Bone Box

The Roundheads climbed to the top of the screen,
prised off the lid and peered inside
then used the bones to smash the coloured glass.
The monks came later and swept up

eight kings of England and a Norman queen,
two princes of the royal blood
where they lay scattered in the nave:
fragments of breastbone and a skull

all jumbled in a gilded chest
no more than thirteen inches wide.
Our task now's not to venerate –
to measure, not to pray,

assisting in the details of the coming miracle –
to reassemble and identify,
to find the reason and the exact date
of finger bone and clavicle;

to shake off the fetters of the grave
so they can rise together and apart
unresisting after their long sleep,
to face the scourging fires of Judgement Day.

Market Street

There is no market now – only the name
and a hundred yards of cobbles
where the tarmac has worn thin

to hint at what was there between the wars:
a ginnel sloping down to the canal,
the clattering of hooves as carts were hauled

to fill the stalls that lined the town.
Like Meadow Bank and Orchard Grove
the name replaces what was there

before we started to forget
like ghost signs fading on the red brick walls.
It is enough to lie here when it rains

through random moments of the night
when something new might still begin –
the curtains drawn, the candles lit

as if the century had never turned
here in the high and bolstered bed
under a canopy of gauze.

The Wall

Is that to keep us out or keep them in?
I asked him with a smile. *That's the best one*
that I've heard all day he said.
It makes no difference either way.
There'll only be one winner in this game.
The gravestones tilted inches from the trench

where he was numbering the stones.
There's six or seven in there mate
as far as I can tell – he cursed
and spat and leaned in on his spade.
They might be my relations I replied.
Another downpour like last night

and you might see them face to face.
I nodded back. *I'll get to see them soon enough* I said
and thought of that lost poet, his long gaze,
the simple fact we can't displace
and what he might have made of this.
But he's long gone and so it falls to me

to watch the slow rebuilding, stone on stone,
and find there's nothing left to say.
See that? He laughed and pointed down the path
where I saw nothing but a belt of winter trees,
the churchyard sloping downhill to the bank
and the river riding roughshod over its still bed.

In the Highlands

A hundred years from now
someone might find
a white, bleached femur

in the purple grass
and further off, perhaps,
a hollow collar bone

picked clean by curlews;
brittle to the touch, exposed –
and pause and let it pass

through all the chambers of the mind
then push on up the mountainside.
We wish for answers to explain

the missing voice, the empty chair
except I think he left them there
to weather and be still

beyond the logic of the maps
where reasons don't exist.
I only know he smiled and waved

then took the less-worn track
where decisions are already made
and in that instant turned to mist.

A Bend in the River

At Putney where the river takes a turn
they crammed into the chancel and the porch,
the smell of death still clinging to their clothes.

Someone sharpened his blunt pen
and dipped it in the ink.
Cromwell, Ireton, Rainsborough

and all the coming men
took turns to shout each other down
between the altar and the pews

and stop the revolution in mid-flow.
And there among the soldiers and their oaths –
the rough-hewn godly of the Civil War,

the stumps of burning candles
and the smell of melting wax,
the bloodstains spreading on the floor

a plain-worded man in a buff-coloured coat
who spoke for us and everyone
and whose name we'll never know.

The Sons of Darkness and the Sons of Light

In the summer of 1977 when I was eighteen I spent a month working on a kibbutz near Jericho. This poem tries to remember that time.

The boy climbed upwards
through a world of death
to find a purchase
on the rocky ledge.
Below him the Dead Sea –
the lowest place on earth;

behind him the Judean Wilderness.
The sun blistered his eyelids,
flaked his lips;
his cracked hands clawed
to reach and grip.
Sheep scurried to the precipice,

dislodging stones.
Up and up he went
into the thin ecstatic air
to shoulder through a crevice
in the rock. The stone he threw
into the silent cave

reverberated in his head;
the false wall crumbled
and the hidden place revealed
the unfurled fragments
in their red clay jars,
the word of Yahweh fine as dust

to sift through fingers,
fall from hands.
Yeshua bar Yoseph
suspended on a beam
between two Zealots
killed for the same crime

while in the city street
a time bomb ticks.
He died renouncing Yahweh
though he called upon his name
over and over as the sky went black.
Up and up we went –

me and the boy who guided me to where
a cairn of shallow stones
marked out the spot.
This is where they buried him he said,
the freedom fighter turning into dust.
They claimed me as their own –

the wilderness, the burning bush,
the hot sun pulsing
where it touches down,
the low rim of that sacred sphere.
I diced the lamb
and cleared a field of stones,

the hot blood sticking to my palms
and in a valley of dry bones
I scrambled through
the nettles and the weeds
and wore a bright star on my chest.
Gone. And in the sterile dust

I rubbed into my hands
I found charred fragments of the past –
a future fixed and certain
as the phases of the moon.
At night I lay unblinking
counting stars to stay awake.

She touched me
and the scales fell from my eyes.
There were angels in the desert
and their hot wings fanned
the bulked and massive
storm clouds from the east.

In the valley of decision
I scraped a circle in the arid sand,
sat in its circuit, prayed for rain.
It didn't come in single drops
but as an inundation
making deep troughs

to irrigate the land.
You curse the fig tree
and denounce the rich,
you heave the tables over
in the Temple portico
and with a plaited whip of cords

drive out the money changers
from their place.
Their coins lie scattered
on the bloodstained floor.
You grapple with Beelzebub
and cast the fallen infidel

into a herd of swine.
All the powers of the world
have set their face against you.
Passover: the first-born snug
in unsuspecting beds,
the lintels daubed with sacrificial blood.

She took me to the well
and made me look
into the darkness
where I saw myself
reflected in the wavering light;
the cool damp recess where

it all began. *Come here
soon and often* she had said,
the sister that I never had,
come here soon and often.
And so I did. I shouted out
my given name

and my name came back to me.
*Your skin is white
but you are one of us.*
Next morning she was gone.
Girl soldiers on the streets
of Bethlehem, guns slung

from shoulders, cracking jokes.
This is where the passion starts:
the rage for justice welling up
into the fallen world,
the radical division that exists
inside the human heart.

I have only one death in me
and the willingness to die,
to let my spirit join them
where the stones are bleached and dry
under the unforgiving sun.
The ruins are more real:

Sepphoris, Caesarea, the city on the hill –
the broken pavements trod, untrod;
the ruined temple
and the toppled synagogue,
the tattoo parlours hid from sight.
This was long before

the mobile phone,
before the laptop
and the world of screens.
I scratched words on a postcard,
sent it home, told my mother
that I loved her. Meanwhile

I was becoming someone else.
A danger, as they told me, to myself.
Don't touch me. Let me go.
James the brother of the Lord
enters the Temple on the Holy Day.
His knees are like a camel's

calloused from the years of prayer.
His hair is oiled and skims
the marble floor.
Nazarite and witness he intones
the sacred words.
The silken curtain parts

and he goes in.
The scent of incense hits him
and he smiles. He knows
that he is holy from the womb,
knows that the stones
will kill him in the end,

the air around him tremulous and blent.
I went down into the empty tomb
beneath the edifice
and felt the weight above me
as I kissed the closed-in walls.
The streets were filled with tourists

and the holy bric-a-brac.
Killer of the prophets
how I wept for you
as I walked your teeming thoroughfares
and bright arcades;
how I noted in the faces

I encountered in the shade
the marks of weakness
and the marks of woe
that led me to the blocks of whitened stone;
that led me to the black-clad figures
wailing at the wall

and rocking to the rhythm of their song.
Each niche and recess
held a scribbled prayer –
a crumpled supplication
for the world to start again.
No stone will be left here upon a stone

and not cast down.
And even now
sometimes I wish I'd stayed
to catch in the low wind
the primal word;
to lie close to the camp fire in the night

and hear the murmuring:
the hidden disputations that occurred
out on the limit, on the edge,
on the border, on the line
between the sons of darkness
and the sons of light.

Acknowledgements

Black Nore Review, Cumbrian Times, Dymock Poets Journal, Scintilla, The Fig Tree, The High Window, The Lake, Northern Gravy, Pennine Platform, Poetry Greece, Poetry Village, Sixty Odd Poets, Starbeck Orion, Strix, Wild Court, Writing Voices, Yorkshire Times.

The Fig Tree Anthology 2024 edited by Tim Fellows.

Coal (Poetry Business) edited by Peter Sansom, Ann Sansom, and Sarah Wimbush.

The Northern Gravy Anthology edited by Ralph Dartford.

The Fig Tree Coal Mining Anthology edited by Tim Fellows.

Bread and Roses Anthology 2022, 2023, 2024 (Culture Matters).

Griffin on Griffin edited by Pamela Scobie.

Some of these poems previously appeared in the limited edition pamphlets *Winter Hill, Milner Place in Heaven,* and in the *New Poems* section of *Selected Poems 1983-2023* (Calder Valley Poetry).

I would like to thank Gladstone's Library for a residency during which some of these poems were started – and Hawkwood College, Stroud for a fellowship during which some of them were finished.

Special thanks are due to Matthew Paul and Tim Fellows, sons of light both, for their invaluable help.